EMMANUEL JOSEPH

The Legacy We Carry, Stories of Family, Community, and the Creative Spark That Endures

Copyright © 2025 by Emmanuel Joseph

All rights reserved. No part of this publication may be reproduced, stored or transmitted in any form or by any means, electronic, mechanical, photocopying, recording, scanning, or otherwise without written permission from the publisher. It is illegal to copy this book, post it to a website, or distribute it by any other means without permission.

First edition

This book was professionally typeset on Reedsy.
Find out more at reedsy.com

Contents

1	Chapter 1: The Call to Adventure	1
2	Chapter 2: The First Steps	3
3	Chapter 3: Embracing the Unknown	5
4	Chapter 4: Building Resilience	6
5	Chapter 5: Learning from Setbacks	8
6	Chapter 6: The Power of Community	9
7	Chapter 7: Finding Joy in the Journey	10
8	Chapter 8: Overcoming Fear	11
9	Chapter 9: Cultivating Curiosity	12
10	Chapter 10: Navigating Challenges	13
11	Chapter 11: The Role of Intuition	14
12	Chapter 12: The Transformative Power of Nature	15
13	Chapter 13: The Art of Letting Go	16
14	Chapter 14: Celebrating Milestones	17
15	Chapter 15: Embracing the Journey's End	18
16	Chapter 16: Sharing Your Story	19
17	Chapter 17: Continuing the Path	20

1

Chapter 1: The Call to Adventure

The dawn of a new adventure always begins with a subtle call. It might be a whisper in the back of your mind or an undeniable urge to break free from the monotony. For some, it's a restless feeling that stirs in the depths of their soul, an insistent yearning for something beyond the ordinary. Others may find their call through an unexpected event, a moment of serendipity that ignites their desire for change.

Take, for example, Sarah, a corporate lawyer who had spent years climbing the professional ladder. She was successful, well-respected, and yet, deep inside, she felt a profound emptiness. It was during a routine commute, staring out of the train window, that she saw a group of backpackers with radiant smiles and a palpable sense of freedom. In that moment, Sarah recognized her call to adventure—a longing to experience life beyond the confines of her office and structured schedule.

Recognizing the call to adventure is the first step on a transformative path. It's about tuning into those subtle signals and understanding that there is more to life than the routines we've grown accustomed to. It requires a willingness to listen to our inner voice and a readiness to embrace the unknown.

However, recognizing the call is not always easy. It often involves overcoming societal expectations and the fear of stepping out of our comfort zones. For many, the call to adventure is drowned out by the noise of daily responsibilities and the pressure to conform. Yet, those who dare to listen find that the rewards are immeasurable. They discover new passions, forge deeper connections, and unlock a wellspring of joy and fulfillment.

This chapter delves into the moments that ignite our desire for change and how recognizing this call can set us on a transformative path. Through real-life examples and personal anecdotes, we'll explore how embracing uncertainty can lead to unexpected joys and profound growth. Sarah's story is just one of many that illustrate the power of answering the call to adventure. Whether it's a career change, a travel expedition, or a personal quest, the journey begins with a single, courageous step.

2

Chapter 2: The First Steps

Starting any journey can be daunting, but every great adventure begins with a single step. It's that initial moment of commitment, the decision to venture into the unknown, that sets the wheels in motion. The first steps are often filled with hesitation and doubt, but they also carry the promise of new experiences and personal growth.

Consider the story of Michael, an engineer who had always dreamed of writing a novel. For years, he had tucked away this aspiration, convinced that his technical background disqualified him from pursuing a creative endeavor. One evening, while browsing through a bookstore, he stumbled upon a writing workshop flyer. Without overthinking it, he signed up, knowing that this small action was the first step toward his dream.

Taking the first steps requires a blend of courage and intention. It's about setting clear goals and creating a roadmap for the journey ahead. This chapter will highlight the importance of establishing a vision for what we hope to achieve and taking practical steps to bring it to life. We'll discuss strategies for overcoming the fear and doubt that often accompany new beginnings.

The initial stages of any adventure are filled with learning and adaptation. Michael's journey into writing was not without its challenges—he faced writer's block, self-doubt, and the daunting task of balancing his new passion with his existing commitments. Yet, each hurdle he overcame brought him closer to his dream. His story reminds us that the path to success is rarely linear, but with perseverance, the rewards are worth the effort.

3

Chapter 3: Embracing the Unknown

As we move further along our path, we must learn to embrace the unknown. The beauty of adventure lies in its unpredictability—the thrill of not knowing what lies ahead. It's in these moments of uncertainty that we discover our true potential and uncover hidden strengths.

The story of Emma, a young artist who decided to travel solo through Southeast Asia, exemplifies this. Leaving behind the familiarity of her hometown, she embarked on a journey with no fixed itinerary. Along the way, she encountered diverse cultures, forged meaningful connections, and discovered a profound sense of independence. Each day brought new challenges and surprises, but it was through embracing the unknown that Emma experienced the most profound growth.

This chapter will explore the beauty of uncertainty and the limitless possibilities it brings. Through stories of adventurers and explorers, we'll see how stepping into the unknown can lead to incredible discoveries and personal revelations. We'll also discuss strategies for staying open and adaptable in the face of unexpected challenges.

Embracing the unknown requires a mindset shift—an acceptance that not everything can be planned or controlled. It's about trusting the journey and allowing ourselves to be vulnerable. Emma's story reminds us that the most memorable and transformative experiences often come from stepping outside our comfort zones and embracing the unexpected.

4

Chapter 4: Building Resilience

Resilience is the backbone of any great journey. It's the quality that allows us to bounce back from setbacks, adapt to changing circumstances, and continue moving forward despite obstacles. Building resilience is essential for navigating the ups and downs of any adventure.

One inspiring example is the story of David, a marathon runner who faced a career-threatening injury. Forced to take a hiatus from running, David was initially devastated. However, instead of succumbing to despair, he focused on rehabilitation and found new ways to stay active. He took up swimming and cycling, eventually transitioning to triathlons. His resilience not only helped him recover but also led him to discover a new passion.

This chapter will delve into the importance of developing mental and emotional strength to withstand the trials and tribulations we encounter along the way. We'll examine techniques for building resilience, such as mindfulness practices, self-care routines, and the power of positive thinking. Real-life examples will illustrate how resilience can help us overcome obstacles and keep moving forward.

Building resilience involves a combination of self-awareness, adaptability, and perseverance. It's about recognizing our strengths and using them to navigate challenges. David's journey highlights the power of resilience in transforming adversity into opportunity. His story encourages us to stay hopeful and determined, even in the face of seemingly insurmountable obstacles.

5

Chapter 5: Learning from Setbacks

Setbacks are an inevitable part of any adventure. No matter how well we plan, there will always be obstacles and unexpected challenges along the way. The key to navigating these setbacks lies in our ability to reframe them as opportunities for growth and learning.

Consider the story of Elena, a passionate chef who dreamed of opening her own restaurant. After months of preparation and planning, she finally opened her doors to the public. However, within the first few weeks, she faced numerous challenges—equipment failures, staffing issues, and negative reviews. At first, Elena felt overwhelmed and discouraged. But instead of giving up, she decided to view each setback as a chance to learn and improve.

Learning from setbacks requires a mindset shift. It's about understanding that failure is not the end, but a part of the journey. This chapter will explore the importance of perseverance and the lessons we can glean from our mistakes. Through inspiring stories of individuals who have turned their setbacks into comebacks, we'll learn how to stay motivated and resilient in the face of adversity.

Elena's journey teaches us that setbacks can be our greatest teachers. By analyzing what went wrong and making necessary adjustments, she was able to turn her restaurant into a thriving success. Her story reminds us that every obstacle we face is an opportunity to grow, adapt, and come back stronger.

6

Chapter 6: The Power of Community

No journey is ever truly a solo endeavor. The support of others can be a crucial element in our success and happiness. This chapter will highlight the importance of community and the support systems we build along the way.

Take the example of Raj, an entrepreneur who embarked on the journey of starting his own tech company. Initially, Raj tried to do everything on his own, believing that he had to prove himself. However, he quickly realized that building a successful business required more than just his individual efforts. He reached out to mentors, joined networking groups, and built a team of like-minded individuals who shared his vision.

The power of community lies in its ability to provide support, encouragement, and diverse perspectives. We'll discuss how connecting with others can enrich our experiences and provide us with the strength and encouragement we need to keep moving forward. Through examples of powerful partnerships and collaborations, we'll see how community can play a pivotal role in our personal growth.

Raj's story illustrates the importance of surrounding ourselves with a supportive network. By leveraging the strengths and insights of others, he was able to overcome challenges and achieve his goals. His experience reminds us that we don't have to navigate our journeys alone—community can be a powerful ally.

7

Chapter 7: Finding Joy in the Journey

Adventure isn't just about the destination; it's about finding joy in the journey itself. It's easy to get caught up in the pursuit of goals and forget to savor the present moment. This chapter will explore the small moments of happiness that can be found along the way.

Consider the story of Lily, a photographer who decided to travel the world capturing breathtaking landscapes. While her ultimate goal was to create a stunning photo book, she discovered that the true joy of her journey lay in the everyday experiences—the conversations with locals, the quiet moments of reflection, and the unexpected encounters with wildlife.

Finding joy in the journey requires mindfulness and gratitude. This chapter will discuss the importance of appreciating the present moment and finding happiness in the little things. Through personal anecdotes and inspiring stories, we'll learn how to savor the journey and find joy in even the most mundane experiences.

Lily's story reminds us that the journey itself can be just as rewarding as the destination. By staying present and mindful, we can experience the richness of life in every moment. Her journey encourages us to find joy in the process and celebrate the beauty of our everyday adventures.

8

Chapter 8: Overcoming Fear

Fear is a constant companion on any adventure, but it doesn't have to hold us back. This chapter will delve into the nature of fear and how we can confront and overcome it.

Take the story of Carlos, a mountaineer who dreamed of summiting Everest. The fear of the unknown, the risk of failure, and the physical challenges were daunting. However, Carlos knew that overcoming fear was essential to achieving his goal. He trained rigorously, sought guidance from experienced climbers, and developed mental strategies to manage his anxiety.

Overcoming fear involves understanding its origins and developing techniques to manage it. This chapter will explore strategies for managing fear, such as exposure therapy, mindfulness practices, and cognitive-behavioral techniques. Through stories of individuals who have faced their fears head-on, we'll learn how to harness the power of fear and turn it into a driving force for growth.

Carlos's journey teaches us that fear is a natural part of any challenge, but it doesn't have to paralyze us. By confronting and embracing our fears, we can push beyond our limits and achieve remarkable feats. His story inspires us to face our own fears with courage and determination.

9

Chapter 9: Cultivating Curiosity

Curiosity is the spark that ignites our desire for adventure. It fuels our passion for exploration and drives us to seek out new experiences. Cultivating curiosity is essential for discovering new opportunities and expanding our horizons.

Consider the story of Amara, a software developer who felt stuck in her routine. She decided to take a sabbatical to explore different cultures and learn new skills. Amara's journey took her to various countries, where she immersed herself in local traditions, learned new languages, and picked up unique skills like pottery and cooking. Her curiosity led her to unexpected adventures and personal growth.

Cultivating curiosity involves being open to new experiences and embracing a mindset of continuous learning. This chapter will explore the importance of cultivating a curious mindset and how it can lead to new discoveries and opportunities. We'll discuss the benefits of lifelong learning and the joy of exploring new interests and passions.

Amara's journey reminds us that curiosity can open doors to unexpected adventures. By staying curious and open-minded, we can uncover new passions and experiences that enrich our lives. Her story encourages us to embrace our curiosity and follow the paths it leads us down.

10

Chapter 10: Navigating Challenges

Every adventure comes with its fair share of challenges. These obstacles test our resolve and push us to grow. Navigating challenges requires resilience, problem-solving skills, and a positive attitude.

Take the story of Liam, a cyclist who set out to complete a cross-country bike tour. Along the way, he faced numerous challenges, from harsh weather conditions to mechanical breakdowns. Despite these setbacks, Liam remained determined to reach his destination. He relied on his problem-solving skills, adaptability, and the support of fellow cyclists to overcome each challenge.

Navigating challenges involves staying focused on our goals and finding creative solutions to the problems we encounter. This chapter will provide practical tips and strategies for navigating the obstacles we face along the way. We'll discuss the importance of problem-solving skills, adaptability, and resourcefulness.

Liam's journey teaches us that challenges are an integral part of any adventure. By staying resilient and resourceful, we can overcome obstacles and continue moving forward. His story inspires us to face our challenges with determination and creativity.

11

Chapter 11: The Role of Intuition

Intuition is a powerful tool that can guide us on our journey. It's that inner voice that helps us make decisions and navigate the unknown. Trusting our intuition can lead us to unexpected opportunities and help us avoid pitfalls.

Consider the story of Maya, an entrepreneur who started her own fashion line. Throughout her journey, Maya relied on her intuition to make important business decisions. Whether it was choosing the right partners, designing new collections, or navigating market trends, her intuition played a crucial role in her success.

Developing and honing our intuition involves mindfulness and self-awareness. This chapter will explore the importance of listening to our inner voice and trusting our instincts. We'll discuss techniques for developing and honing our intuition, such as meditation and mindfulness practices.

Maya's story illustrates the power of intuition in guiding us on our journey. By trusting our inner voice, we can make informed decisions and navigate the unknown with confidence. Her experience encourages us to develop and rely on our intuition as we embark on our adventures.

12

Chapter 12: The Transformative Power of Nature

Nature has a profound ability to heal and transform us. It provides a sense of peace, inspiration, and connection that can enhance our adventure. Spending time in nature can rejuvenate our spirits and help us gain perspective.

Consider the story of Alex, a stressed-out executive who decided to take a break from his demanding job. He embarked on a solo hiking trip in the mountains, where he spent days immersed in the natural world. The experience allowed him to disconnect from the chaos of his everyday life and reconnect with himself. He returned from his trip with a renewed sense of clarity and purpose.

The transformative power of nature lies in its ability to provide solace and inspiration. This chapter will delve into the benefits of spending time in nature and how it can enhance our adventure. We'll discuss the importance of connecting with the natural world and the ways in which it can inspire and rejuvenate us.

Alex's journey highlights the healing and transformative power of nature. By immersing ourselves in the natural world, we can find solace and inspiration that enriches our lives. His story encourages us to seek out nature and embrace its healing potential.

13

Chapter 13: The Art of Letting Go

Sometimes, the greatest adventure is learning to let go. The art of letting go involves releasing what no longer serves us and embracing change. It requires courage and a willingness to trust the process.

Consider the story of Nina, a woman who had been holding onto a toxic relationship for years. Despite the red flags, she clung to the hope that things would improve. One day, she realized that holding on was preventing her from finding true happiness. With a heavy heart, she decided to let go and start anew. This decision marked the beginning of a transformative journey that led her to rediscover herself and find joy in unexpected places.

Letting go involves understanding that change is a natural part of life and that holding on to the past can hinder our growth. This chapter will explore techniques for letting go, such as forgiveness practices and decluttering our lives. We'll discuss the importance of making space for new opportunities and experiences.

Nina's story reminds us that letting go can be a liberating and empowering experience. By releasing what no longer serves us, we create room for growth and new beginnings. Her journey encourages us to trust the process and embrace the changes that come our way.

14

Chapter 14: Celebrating Milestones

Every adventure has its milestones worth celebrating. These moments of achievement and progress are important markers on our journey. Celebrating milestones allows us to reflect on how far we've come and appreciate the hard work and effort that got us there.

Take the story of Ethan, a musician who dreamed of recording his own album. After years of practice, dedication, and countless gigs, he finally achieved his goal. Instead of rushing to the next project, Ethan took the time to celebrate this milestone with his friends and family. The celebration not only boosted his motivation but also reminded him of the support and love that had fueled his journey.

Celebrating milestones involves acknowledging our achievements and taking the time to appreciate our progress. This chapter will discuss different ways to mark our milestones, from personal rituals to communal celebrations. We'll explore the importance of gratitude and the impact of celebrating our successes.

Ethan's story highlights the significance of celebrating milestones. By taking the time to honor our achievements, we boost our motivation and remind ourselves of the support and effort that have contributed to our success. His journey encourages us to celebrate our progress and appreciate the moments that define our adventure.

15

Chapter 15: Embracing the Journey's End

Every journey eventually comes to an end, but that doesn't mean the adventure is over. Embracing the conclusion of our journey involves reflecting on the lessons we've learned and the growth we've experienced.

Consider the story of Sam, a teacher who decided to retire after decades of inspiring students. As he packed up his classroom for the last time, Sam reflected on the countless lives he had touched and the lessons he had imparted. While he felt a sense of nostalgia, he also embraced the new opportunities that retirement would bring—time for travel, hobbies, and spending time with loved ones.

Embracing the journey's end involves gratitude and reflection. This chapter will explore the importance of acknowledging the impact of our journey and the ways in which our experiences have shaped us. We'll discuss the transition from one adventure to the next and how to carry forward the lessons we've learned.

Sam's story reminds us that the end of one journey can be the beginning of another. By embracing the conclusion of our adventures, we create space for new experiences and opportunities. His journey encourages us to reflect on our growth and appreciate the impact of our journey.

16

Chapter 16: Sharing Your Story

Our adventures have the power to inspire others. Sharing our stories allows us to create ripples of positive change and connect with those around us. It can be a source of inspiration, encouragement, and support.

Take the story of Olivia, a cancer survivor who decided to share her journey through a blog. By openly discussing her challenges, triumphs, and lessons learned, she provided hope and support to countless others facing similar battles. Her story resonated with readers worldwide, creating a community of individuals who found strength and inspiration in her words.

Sharing our stories involves being vulnerable and authentic. This chapter will discuss the importance of sharing our experiences and the impact they can have on those around us. We'll explore different ways to share our stories, from writing and speaking to mentoring and teaching.

Olivia's journey illustrates the power of storytelling. By sharing her experiences, she created a supportive community and inspired others to face their challenges with courage and resilience. Her story encourages us to share our own adventures and connect with others in meaningful ways.

17

Chapter 17: Continuing the Path

The end of one adventure is just the beginning of another. Our journey of self-discovery and growth is a lifelong pursuit filled with endless possibilities. Embracing new challenges and setting new goals allows us to continue carving our unique path.

Consider the story of Tom, an artist who, after completing a successful career in painting, decided to explore sculpture. With a heart full of curiosity and a willingness to learn, Tom embarked on a new creative journey. His passion for exploration and growth led him to discover new dimensions of his artistic expression.

Continuing the path involves embracing a mindset of lifelong learning and growth. This final chapter will discuss the importance of setting new goals and embracing new challenges. Through inspiring stories, we'll see how the uncarved path is a lifelong journey filled with endless possibilities for adventure, resilience, and joy.

Tom's journey reminds us that our adventures are never truly over. By continuously seeking new challenges and opportunities, we keep our spirits alive and our paths ever-evolving. His story encourages us to embrace the endless possibilities that life has to offer and continue our journey of self-discovery and growth.

The Uncarved Path: Rediscovering Yourself Through Adventure, Resilience, and Joy

CHAPTER 17: CONTINUING THE PATH

Embark on a transformative journey with "The Uncarved Path," a captivating exploration of self-discovery and personal growth. Through a series of inspiring stories and practical insights, this book guides readers on a quest to rediscover their true selves by embracing adventure, building resilience, and finding joy in the journey.

In this book, you'll encounter real-life examples of individuals who have answered the call to adventure and navigated the uncharted territories of their lives. From overcoming fear and setbacks to celebrating milestones and embracing change, each chapter delves into the challenges and triumphs that define the human experience.

Discover the power of community, the beauty of the unknown, and the art of letting go as you journey through the pages of "The Uncarved Path." With each chapter, you'll uncover valuable lessons and practical tips for navigating your own adventure with courage, curiosity, and an open heart.

Whether you're seeking inspiration for a new beginning or looking to reignite your passion for life, "The Uncarved Path" offers a roadmap to rediscovering your true potential. Embrace the uncarved path and find the resilience, joy, and fulfillment that await you on this extraordinary journey.